THE CASE OF
Erle Stanley Gardner

THE CASE OF

Erle Stanley Gardner

BY

ALVA JOHNSTON

WILLIAM MORROW & COMPANY
NEW YORK

ILLUSTRATIONS

THE CASE OF
Erle Stanley Gardner

ERLE STANLEY GARDNER, the creator of Perry Mason, is the king of the pocket libraries and the people's choice for America's greatest living writer. His mysteries, in all editions from two dollars to twenty-five cents, had total sales of 4,547,922 in 1943, and 4,903,685 in 1944, and 6,104,000 in 1945.

Up to May 1st of the year 1946, one publisher of pocket-sized books sold 13,146,520 Gardner books—$3,286,630 worth at twenty-five cents apiece. *The Case of the Curious Bride* led the list with 1,336,907. The million mark was topped by four others—*The Case of the Counterfeit Eye, The Case of the Stuttering Bishop, The Case of the Lame Canary* and *The Case of the Substitute Face. The Bigger They Come*, a Donald Lam-Bertha Cool mystery by A. A. Fair, which is another name for Erle Stanley Gardner, has passed the three-quarter-million mark. *The D.A. Calls It Murder*, a Gardner story about the prosecutor hero, Douglas Selby, has passed the half-million mark. Another publisher of pocket-sized books has sold more than a million Donald Lam-Bertha Cool mysteries. Gardner's books circulate like currency. He probably has the greatest lending-library and book-swapping public in the country. His readers are computed by the tens of millions.

Most writers write for fame and money. Gardner wrote to go hunting. In 1923, when he wrote *The Shrieking Skeleton*, his first novelette for a pulp magazine, he was a thirty-four-year-old lawyer of Ventura, California, and locally famous as a courtroom gladiator. But the law kept interfering with his hunting trips. Three times he had started for Alaska for big game. Each trip was interrupted by telegrams urging him to hustle back to Ventura to handle important trials. The judges of several California counties got tired of tearing their court calendars to pieces and rearranging them to suit young Nimrod's hunting schedule. Erle's partners wore themselves out begging other lawyers to postpone trials until Erle got back from the elk, caribou and wild-pig country.

Erle loved the law, but he loved outdoor life better. He looked around for an occupation which would allow him to work when and where he pleased. He arrived at the conclusion that there were only two such occupations—the mail-order business and story writing. He tried mail order first, establishing a correspondence school which gave lawyers a series of easy lessons in how to look their clients in the eye and charge them adequate fees. One hundred letters were sent out to lawyers, and the responses showed that the legal profession was hungry for such instruction. But, after considerable study, Erle reached the conclusion that the mail-order business would tie him down, and that fiction was the only free way of life.

To this day, Erle's partners and some other early associates think that he made the wrong decision. Jerry Giesler, of Los Angeles, probably the most noted courtroom warrior in America, has stated that Erle would have been one of the greatest trial lawyers in the country, if he had stayed with the law. Judge Louis C. Drapeau, of the Superior Court of Ventura County, a former partner of Erle's, has boldly declared that Erle, if he had only stuck to his first profession, would have developed into a second

Garret W. McEnerney—the Daniel Webster of California. They say in Ventura that Erle was a master of logic, a born cross-examiner and a magician at the technical witchcraft of the law.

Gardner never repented of his decision to quit the law in favor of writing. He has succeeded pretty well in getting the life he wanted. He takes things easy at his 400-acre Rancho del Paisano near Temecula in Southern California, dictates only five or six novels and a few score radio scripts a year, ropes cattle on a 96,000-acre ranch adjoining his property, goes on a hunting trip with his bow and arrows when he feels like it, and strikes out for other parts of the world when the spirit moves him.

He is a young-looking man for his fifty-seven years. He is of middle height, but so broad across the chest and shoulders that he seems short. His arms are not quite long enough for his extra-wide physique, and this causes him to handle his bow and arrows in an unorthodox manner that is criticized by experts. But, in spite of his inelegant technique, he has killed an elk and brought in quail for breakfast with his bow and arrows. He does all his hunting nowadays with these primitive weapons. His study or dictating cabin at Rancho del Paisano looks like a world's-fair exhibit of archery.

Gardner has a broad, somewhat weather-beaten face, a shock of brown hair and gold-mounted spectacles. His favorite phrase in describing Perry Mason is "thought-slitted eyes," and this is one of many of his own characteristics which the author has transferred to his hero. Erle's legal associates say that hostile witnesses used to break down under his accusing squint. It was supposed to have the effect of a sharpshooter drawing a bead on the prevari-

11

cating centers of the brain. Earl Rogers, the tyrannosaur of the Southern California bar, used to whip out a lorgnette to X-ray the souls of witnesses. The Ventura authorities say that, by merely contracting his lids, Erle was able to see the lies swarming around in a man's brain like bees in a glass-enclosed hive. Agents and others who have business relations with him say it is impossible to get noncommittal with Erle. He fixes his nickel-in-the-slot eyes on them, peers into the back of their minds, shoots rapid-fire questions at them and pulls their mental reservations out by the roots.

The oratorical muscles of Erle's cheeks and neck have a herculean development from scores of millions of words barked in court and rattled off into a recording machine. His voice detonates with authority. In dictating one Perry Mason courtroom scene Erle said, "Court dismissed," with such a peremptory snarl that a new secretary, on hearing the words reproduced by a wax cylinder, closed up her desk and called it a day.

Gardner has a split personality—half mixer, half hermit. He bought his ranch for its comparative inaccessibility, but it has grown into a resort and recreation center. He now has eight houses scattered among fine old oaks on a hillside commanding a broad sweep of landscape. He still refuses to install a telephone, but he is a gold mine to the telegraph office at Temecula. Western Union operators in far-off cities are acquainted with the Erle Stanley Gardner situation and will volunteer the information that there is an extra charge for a telegram to him because they have to be delivered to his ranch by special couriers. It takes three secretaries to handle Erle's endless chain of dictated records. The chief of these is Miss Jean Bethell, who has been with him for more than twenty years and has for thirteen years been sitting for the literary portrait of Della Street, Perry Mason's secretary. The main recreations on the ranch are horseback riding and bow-and-arrow golf, a sport in which arrows serve as golf balls, and transfixing a paper bag is the equivalent of sinking a putt. When his guest cabins are filled, Erle frequently gets up at four A.M. and dictates five or ten thousand words before breakfast. He busies himself with a stable of horses and a few cattle, and is often engaged in nursing orphaned coyote whelps and other distressed animals and birds. The place is a Mecca for the disinherited mongrels of the region.

When distractions become too numerous, Erle gets out his command car and sets out for his second line of defense against civilization—his inaccessible cabin on his other ranch, 1400 acres on the backbone of the Coast Range. There he settles down among his own private mountains and his own private canyons under his own private sky, and dictates to the machine from dawn until sundown, when he lights up his kerosene lamp and continues to dictate. He likes housekeeping in an isolated one-man establishment. Whenever a lone prospector or solitary cabin dweller wanders into one of his plots, Erle gets into a glow and begins to write like a lodge brother about a charter member. A man who has got hundreds of millions of words off his chest in his lifetime, Erle idolizes the say-nothing-to-nobody fellows who commune with nature in the desert and in the high Sierras. His most appetizing gastronomic passages are about beans fresh from the can cooked up with onions and garlic. After a spell of solitude in his mountain aerie, Erle comes back with a command car full of records and is the life of the party again.

Erle did not give up his legal work when he sold his first story to *Black Mask* in 1923. For nearly ten years he practiced law by day and literature by night. He handled the most important courtroom trials of his career while producing pulp fiction at the rate of a million words a year. In 1932, he dictated his first Perry Mason novel, *The Case of the Velvet Claws*, in three days and a half, while devoting part of each day to his practice. In its fourteenth year, old *Velvet Claws* still has a flourishing sale in twenty-five-cent, forty-nine-cent and seventy-five-cent editions, and enjoys the status of an incipient classic.

After doing his first novel at a sprint, Erle slowed down to the jog trot of a week to a book. In recent years he has dawdled away as much as a month on one book.

His greatest contribution to letters at a given stretch—224,000 words in one month in 1932—took place while he was still working two days a week for the law firm of Sheridan, Drapeau, Orr and Gardner. In his furious campaign for freedom and leisure, he got along with as little as three hours' sleep a night.

There have been criticisms to the effect that his work shows signs of haste, but this is irrelevant fault-finding. What Erle's public wants from him is not artistic finish, but productivity. The true Gardner fan wants more Gardner, not better Gardner. Their demand is that he brace up and quit babying himself and turn out twelve novels a year instead of six.

Will Cuppy, the Longinus and Quintilian of mystery critics, has complained that Gardner uses the same formula too often. In most detective stories, characters are twisted like Monterey cypresses and probability is fearfully maltreated, because of the iron rules of the mystery. No literary form except the sonnet is governed by such inflexible laws. At the last minute a magical solution must be pulled out of the hat, proving that the reader misunderstood everything and everybody all along. In the Perry Mason stories, Gardner has a formula within a formula. Not only must there be a surprise solution at the end, but that solution must be brought about by Perry's cross-examination of witnesses in a courtroom. It is also practically a statutory requirement that Perry, in his unparalleled services for his clients, should get himself in dire peril of being arrested as an accessory after the fact and of being hauled up before the grievance committee of the Bar Association. The result is that, while Erle invents an endless diversity of detail, a sameness of pattern runs through most of Perry's exploits. But the charge against the average mystery writer is that he resembles mystery writers too much. Erle is accused of resembling only himself.

One source of Gardner's popularity is undoubtedly the average American's fondness for legal problems. Erle has a nation of amateur lawyers from whom to draw his public. We love nothing so much as the law, except seeing it beaten. The county courthouse is the original center of mass entertainment in America. The big trial lawyers are among the most fascinating peacetime heroes. Belasco said that nothing on the stage ever equaled the drama of a murder trial. Crime is best, but the civil law is also fascinating at every turn.

In the variegated practice of a small-town lawyer, Gardner had the whole gamut of criminal cases from murderers to sellers of Chinese lottery tickets. His civil practice ranged from oil litigation and will contests to replevining a sorrel horse with white fetlocks and getting out injunctions to restrain a big black dog from pawing up a newly seeded lawn. When Perry Mason's clients get into jams, Erle still plows through stacks of legal volumes in order to line up the authorities behind Perry's legal acrobatics. He has an extensive law library at his Rancho del Paisano, and a large array of works on criminology, psychiatry and medical jurisprudence. Erle does his best to keep Perry Mason letter-perfect in the law and up-to-date in scientific crime-detection methods. He never lets Perry take a case outside of California. Erle knows California law and California court procedure, and he won't risk being tripped by novel rules of evidence or trick statutes in other states.

Erle has received high recognition for the soundness of his fictionized law. "His court scenes are authentic," wrote John C. Arnold, vice-president of the Pennsylvania Bar, in the *Pennsylvania Bar Association Quarterly* published in January, 1942.

The late Dr. John H. Wigmore, law dean of North-western University and perhaps the most quoted of recent authorities on evidence, said in a fan letter to Erle: "Your *The D.A. Calls It Murder* is your high-water mark, I venture to think. Not only does the plot unfold to a satisfactory (not a forced) solution, but the character sketches give the story a solid permanence in good literature."

Professor Wigmore scoffed, however, at a "perfect murder" theory which Erle, writing under the name of A. A. Fair, put forward in *The Bigger They Come*. This perfect murder was not a matter of manipulating the clues so as to deceive the police, but of juggling two states into an unbreakable jurisdictional deadlock. Donald Lam, the hero, buys an automobile in Arizona with a bad check and then drives the car into California. The automobile dealer procures Donald's extradition from California to Arizona. There Donald pays for the car, convinces the authorities that the bad check was an inadvertence and squares the case. Then he confesses that he is the man who recently committed a sensational murder in California. California seeks to extradite him. Donald flashes a lot of authorities to show that, in order to be extradited, a man must be a fugitive from justice; and that he is not a fugitive, since he was forcibly transported into Arizona. Erle, who never hesitates to throw the law books at his readers, causes his character to argue as follows before the Arizona judge:

"The case of In re Whittington, 34C.A.344, is a leading case and is absolutely in point. I can also refer you to the case of People v. Jones, 54C.A.344. The California doctrine has been succinctly expressed in Volume 12, California Jurisprudence, Page 398, as follows: 'Where it appears that the presence of the accused in the state of refuge is not due to any voluntary act of his own, but to legal or illegal compulsion, he is not a fugitive from justice and cannot be extradited as such.'"

The fictionized Arizona judge sustained this reasoning and the character went scot-free. Professor Wigmore objected to the whole proceeding. He said that the man was essentially a fugitive from justice who had tried to make the courts aid and abet his fugitiveness. Erle submitted an exhaustive brief to his celebrated fan. Professor Wigmore, while not satisfied, admitted that the alleged loophole in the law had greater possibilities than he had at first supposed. But the perfect murderer had better watch his step. The courts have a way of eating their own words from time to time, and they couldn't be trusted to give a square deal to a perfect murderer. Incidentally, it turned out that

17

Detective Donald Lam didn't commit the California murder after all. His confession was a slick ruse to throw the real murderer off guard and bring him to justice.

The Perry Mason books have taught law to lawyers. *The Case of the Curious Bride* is one which has served as a text-book. The curious bride was caught in a net of circumstances which made her look guilty of murder. Her husband told the most damaging story against her, but the wise old law refuses to give man and wife the power to hang each other. The district attorney tried to get around the ancient rule by starting to annul the marriage, so that the husband would be free to take the stand. He made out a prima-facie case that the curious bride was not a bride, by showing that the marriage had taken place before she had received her final divorce papers from Husband No. 1. Then Perry Mason stepped in and proved that Husband No. 1 already had a wife when he went through the ceremony with the curious bride. Not being married to No. 1, she didn't have to be divorced from him. She was, therefore, the lawfully wedded lady of her current spouse, and he was not permitted to enter the witness box against her.

One night in 1941, Darrel R. Parker, of Phoenix, Arizona, chief deputy prosecutor of Maricopa County, was lying in bed reading *The Case of the Curious Bride*. It suddenly occurred to him that the annulment device might be used in the case of Frank Pass, who was accused of murdering Sai Han Ong, a Chinese grocer, with a hammer. The strongest story against Pass was that told by his recent bride, Mrs. Ruby Contreras Pass. The prosecutor had assumed that he couldn't use her testimony, but, after reading the Perry Mason story, he decided to look into the matter further. The Arizona law forbids the marriage of a Caucasian to a person of Indian blood. Pass was one-eighth Paiute Indian, and that rendered him incapable of contracting a legal marriage with a Caucasian. Ruby was legally a Caucasian. In fact, she was half Mexican, but the Arizona law makes the wild assumption that all Mexicans are Caucasians. At the trial the prosecutor called Ruby to the stand. The defense lawyer objected. The prosecutor introduced proof that Pass was 12½ per cent Paiute. The court then ruled that that rendered the marriage null and void, and Ruby gave her testimony. Pass received a sentence of fifteen years to life, and the conviction was upheld on appeal. Prosecutor Parker told newspapermen that he had taken the tip from Erle Stanley Gardner, and the Arizona newspaper account always called the Pass trial The Case of the Curious Bride.

Prosecutor Parker said that Gardner's stories are "always plausible, even to a lawyer," and he added, "Since I first became interested in his work, I have given particular attention to the aspects of criminal law and criminal procedure which constitute a good part of the material of his narrative, and I have yet to detect any situation in which his protagonist has taken a position in the course of a criminal proceeding which would be untenable to the average lawyer familiar with this phase of jurisprudence."

Some critics have questioned whether any lawyer was ever as smart as Perry Mason. But fiction is a weak sister in comparison with truth, as far as the exploits of great jury pleaders are concerned. Erle would be condemned for delirious sensationalism if he credited Perry Mason with feats equal to some of the actual accomplishments of the top courtroom athletes. The late Samuel Untermyer, of New

York, was once assigned to defend a woman after she had made a confession and entered a plea of guilty of murder in the second degree. She had killed her husband by driving a carving knife into his back because he criticized her for entertaining seafaring men in his absence. Changing the plea to not guilty and using the theory that the husband, snarling like a tiger, had charged back-foremost at her with homicidal fury, Untermyer so worked on the jury's feelings that they not only acquitted the little woman but took up a collection in the jury room and presented her with a purse of $100. In a libel suit, Delphin M. Delmas, of California, defended the San Francisco *Call* with such eloquence that one of the jurors held out for hours to convict the plaintiff. Rufus Choate was such a famous acquitter that the pirates of Boston stipulated in their contracts that, if they were caught, old Choate would be hired to defend them.

Some of Erle's own courtroom triumphs would be condemned as improbable fictions if he made use of them in the Perry Mason stories. During a will case in Ventura, a local psychiatric expert folded up under Erle's questioning. The expert testified that he had treated the testator and that the man was undoubtedly crazy at the time when he made the will. The expert was a surprise witness. Erle had to improvise his cross-examination on the spot. Calling on his memory, which was well stocked with psychiatric stuff from earlier law cases, Erle began to ask learned questions. The expert showed signs of wavering when he was asked about the "neurodendrite" and the "neurologic theory of thought."

"Do you know the relation of the synapsis of the neurodendrons to judgment?" asked the lawyer.

"Yes, but I won't discuss it," said the expert.

As Erle proceeded to examine him about the "basket cells," the expert turned to the judge and asked to be excused. He said that, although he had once been the head of a large psychiatric institution, he had not kept up with recent developments and had decided that he did not want to be an expert. The judge dismissed the will contest and decided in favor of Erle's clients.

Frank Orr, one of Erle's Ventura partners, said that on one occasion when Erle was pitted against an important Los Angeles law firm in a trial in Los Angeles, Erle manhandled a big-time medical expert so severely that, just after the judge declared a recess, the bailiff exclaimed, "It looks like the country boy is making monkeys of the city boys."

A severe earthquake hit the Ventura courthouse on February 18, 1926, when Erle was cross-examining a young woman who had sued a client of Erle's for $250,000. She said that Erle's client had slandered her, preventing her marriage and making her a nervous wreck. The young woman had been told that her sole chance of winning the verdict depended on avoiding Lawyer Gardner's traps, and that she must keep her head during the cross-examination. She had been handling herself pretty well up to the time when the temblor, as they call it in Southern California, began to rock the courtroom. Then she did too well. Erle paid no attention to the quake, and neither did she. "Jurymen and spectators were showing an inclination to strike out for the door," according to the account in the Ventura Daily *Post*. The woman's lawyer dived behind a chair. Another man crawled under a table. But the rhythm of the cross-examination was not even disturbed.

Erle kept putting questions, and the witness answered them without missing a beat. Finally the judge rapped with his gavel, said, "Court recessed," and the courtroom emptied in record time.

In an ordinary case the witness would have been open to congratulations for her display of iron nerve. But what she had forgotten was that she wasn't supposed to have an iron nerve. Her nervous system was supposed to have been shattered.

"You jurymen were nervous enough," said Erle, in his address to the jury. "The spectators were nervous enough. I never saw a more nervous man than her big two-hundred-pound lawyer, who tried to hide behind a chair. But here she sat throughout the earthquake, answering questions composedly and without a tremor. She was as cool as a cucumber. We ought all to have nervous breakdowns if they cause such wonderful calmness and poise."

It took the jury fifteen minutes to bring in a verdict in favor of Erle's client.

Erle carried many of his cases up to the State Supreme Court and sometimes beyond. One of these was the case of a Mexican named Joseph Sandoval, who had been convicted of murder and sentenced to be hanged. Erle had not represented him at the trial. His sympathies had been aroused when he heard Sandoval's statement to the court before sentence was pronounced. When the conviction was upheld by the higher courts, Erle took over the case at his own expense and obtained a rehearing by the California Supreme Court by a trick legal writ called a *coram nobis*. The court complimented Erle for the humanity he had displayed in his exertions for Sandoval, but decided that there was no legal ground for a new trial and that the man must hang. That didn't stop Erle. He stirred up the Mexican consul in Los Angeles and the Mexican community of Southern California into an outcry for fair play for Sandoval. He got the twelve jurors who had brought in the verdict of guilty to sign pleas for clemency. He worked up such an agitation that Governor Friend Richardson commuted the sentence to life imprisonment. Sandoval is now free and living the life of a good citizen.

In working at his own expense for another penniless murderer, Erle appealed to the highest California court and lost. By all the rules, that should have ended it. Nevertheless, Erle tried an after-the-bell appeal on grounds that were practically invisible through any legal microscope. He had a deep scheme in the back of his head. He hoped to keep the case juggling around in the courts until after the date set for the hanging, and he expected that the execution would be delayed until the second appeal was decided. He had found some obscure law under which it was illegal to postpone a hanging because of a second appeal. He planned to charge that state officials had neglected to hang the man on the right date and that they had no authority to hang him on an open date of their own choosing. It was to be the legal version of "Curfew shall not ring tonight!" and Erle had some hope of putting his new appeal technique on a perpetual basis. The seven judges of the court of last resort developed a suspicion that they were being trifled with, and they appeared to be pretty bored with Erle. Part of his argument was based on an old decision of that very court. Erle had committed it to memory, and he gave it word for word without stating the source.

"Young man," interrupted one of the judges, "that is the

most puerile reasoning that I have ever heard in all my years on the bench."

"It may be, your honor, but it is the exact language of this court," said Gardner.

He was starting to name the volume and page where the decision would be found, when one judge snapped, "Sit down."

Then another judge snapped, "Sit down."

Then all seven of them chorused, "Sit down."

The presiding judge had a coughing spell, but it was later said that he was covering up a fit of laughter. The seven then went into their chambers and ordered Erle's client to be hanged, and he was hanged. The California legislature at its next session made a thorough revision of the law on death sentences, appeals and hangings, in the hope of preventing legal technicians from discovering any other inviting loopholes.

E RLE STANLEY (Perry Mason) GARDNER didn't know the first thing about writing when, in 1923, he decided to grind out fiction.

He was thirty-four years old. His face had been wedged in lawbooks during a large part of his life, but he had rarely read a novel or short story. Nevertheless, he became a mass producer of fiction after one of the briefest literary apprenticeships on record.

Erle led off by selling two jokes for one dollar apiece and two humorous sketches for fifteen dollars apiece. Then he wrote a novelette, *The Shrieking Skeleton*, and sent it to *Black Mask*, a pulp magazine published in New York City. The manuscript was promptly returned to Erle. Attached to it was the following note which P. C. Cody, circulation manager of *Black Mask*, had written to the editors: "This is the most puerile story I have ever read. The plot has whiskers like Spanish moss on a Southern live oak, and the characters talk like a dictionary."

That was just the thing to fill Erle with enthusiasm. He went back to his typewriter and rewrote *The Shrieking Skeleton* until he had stone bruises on his finger tips. Putting adhesive tape on them, he kept pounding away. He studied and restudied the manuscript, asking himself, "Now have I got all the puerility out of it?" He couldn't tell. A puerile writer has no way of knowing when he is puerile. Erle rewrote every sentence on suspicion.

He kept shooting the plot to pieces and rebuilding it in the hope of knocking the antiquity out of it. He got stone bruises on his brain trying to figure out what Circulation Manager Cody meant by saying that the characters talked like a dictionary. It was common knowledge that everybody used words that were in the dictionary. The fact is so notorious that Homer Dodge, the Washington journalist, once worked on a plan to sign up the heirs of Noah Webster and sue everybody for plagiarism.

At length Erle concluded that he used too many of the long words that send readers running to the dictionary. He had always thought that was what literary style consisted of. It hurt him to do it, but he laboriously translated many of his most cherished sentences into everyday language.

Erle discovered that, like many lawyers, he had two styles—a judge style and a jury style. In arguments to the bench, lawyers can do their hair-splitting better with polysyllables of Latin derivation, but they generally find it is wiser to use Anglo-Saxon on the twelve laymen. Before he was through, Erle had practically changed *The Shrieking Skeleton* from a Supreme Court brief to a jury plea.

All through his subsequent writing career, Erle turned his legal knowledge into a literary bonanza. His second profession has been largely a matter of working up the raw materials of the first. Many of his forty novels and 400 novelettes are law cases that escape from their calf-bound volumes and run amuck.

His very first effort contained a beautiful legal problem. The chief character in *The Shrieking Skeleton* is the great scientist, Doctor Potter, who drives his enemy, Crothers, to a pauper's death, then buys the body, fixes up the skeleton and hangs it in his study so that he can gloat over it when he needs relaxation after stupendous scientific labors. But a nephew of Crothers turns up and demands that uncle be buried. Doctor Potter asks a lawyer named Walter Pearce if the law can step in and rob a hard-working scientist of his only fun.

The lawyer renders the opinion that no man owns his own skeleton; that, in the eyes of the law, a man's skeleton is not an asset; that it cannot be attached or levied upon; that it cannot be bequeathed or inherited; that it is legally the property of the state. Therefore, the nephew, in the capacity of a nephew, cannot disturb Doctor Potter in the peaceful enjoyment of the bones of his old enemy. On the other hand, the lawyer doubts that Doctor Potter acquired a perfect title to the skeleton from the public authorities. Therefore, the nephew, in the capacity of a citizen, can make serious trouble.

Suddenly the skeleton begins to shriek, and the lawyer loses all enthusiasm for the fine points of the case. Doctor Potter is found stabbed through the heart, and the skeleton is accused of pulling a knife on him. Later it appears that the Japanese butler, Kumi, under cover of darkness, had impersonated the skeleton with the aid of phosphorous paint. He wanted to get military secrets on which the scientist was working and to avenge his sister, whom Doctor Potter had wronged while passing through Tokyo twenty years earlier.

Joe E. Brown was a performer in a circus before he was a spectator at one. Broadly speaking, Erle was a producer of fiction before he was a consumer of it. There is evidence, however, that he had hastily tuned up his style on Edgar Allan Poe and a few pulp stories before finishing *The Shrieking Skeleton*. Many of the pulp writers wouldn't use the cold, dead phrase "He said." Those lifeless "He saids" reversed the current and let the juice out of the half-electrocuted reader. When a typical pulp character spoke, he "rasped," "hoarsed" or "shrilled." In his maiden effort, Erle made the grade with "He jerked," "He rapped out" and "He soothed."

In its final revision, *The Shrieking Skeleton* was not only accepted by *Black Mask* but was made the leading story in the issue of December 15, 1923. Erle received a check for $140, a cent a word for 14,000 words, and he was the proudest man in Southern California.

Erle's apprenticeship was now over and he was a full-fledged prose industrialist. He sent for an autographed photo of his benefactor, P. C. Cody, who in two sentences had given him criticism enough to last a lifetime. Erle was soon stamping out one novelette every three days in the time he could spare from his exciting law practice at Ventura, California.

Ring Lardner once advised young writers that the short cut to success was to provide themselves with a lot of colored pencils. Erle preferred an electrically operated typewriter and, later, a recording machine. He has always asserted that he had no "native literary ability," and that anybody can become a good writer by dogged industry. He rates his "native abilities" as follows: as a lawyer very good; as a business analyst, good; as a writer, zero. It is doubtful, however, if "native abilities" can be catalogued like one-purpose machinery—good for printing, but not for hay baling; excellent for concrete mixing, but no good for permanent waves. Erle had the energy of a bursting dam and got about equal results whether he surged into law, business or fiction.

The lack of early literary training might have been a handicap to a manufacturer of epic poems, but not to the Henry Ford of detective mysteries. While he had picked up very little of the rich second-hand stuff of literature, Erle's mind was an animated library of material absorbed from legal broils, business adventures, mining, hunting, yachting, boxing, traveling, amateur photography and amateur astronomy. Both as a lawyer and as a salesman, he had made a living out of applied psychology. He had acquired what has been called the learned spirit of human dealings, and books of his, which would otherwise be machine-made mysteries, take on life as he pours in details which have the authentic ring of experience.

Erle had the further advantage of being born under a wrong-headed star. He narrowly missed becoming a professional againster, and he still throws a somewhat baleful eye at civilization. He had his own private philosophies and a rampant underdog complex. Even when he wrote jig-saw mysteries at the rate of 20,000 words a day, he often succeeded in getting some of his extravagant, highly specialized personality into his pages.

Erle was born at Malden, Massachusetts, on July 17, 1889. His father, Charles W. Gardner, was a mining engineer and an expert in gold dredging. Erle got his early education in snatches at Malden; Falkner, Mississippi; Portland, Oregon; Oroville, California, and Palo Alto, California. He quit one school after another to follow his father to promising beds of gold-bearing gravel. In 1906 he spent several months in the Klondike.

After the Klondike, Erle went to high school at Oroville, California. He wouldn't take any nonsense from the school authorities and was expelled for spending too much time cartooning a long-chinned disciplinarian. His Oroville idol was "Swede" Meyerhoffer, who later became famous as a pioneer stunt flier and was killed in a plane crash. Meyerhoffer took a fancy to Erle and announced that he was going to make a prize fighter of him. He took great pains with Erle and turned him into a pretty good gladiator. One day Erle heard an ambulance clanging along the main street of Oroville. It picked up a man who had rocketed out of a window of the Butte Athletic Club, which Meyerhoffer had founded. The human projectile had been powered by an uppercut from a promising young battler who had been imported from Sacramento to meet Erle in a four-round bout at the Oroville Opera House two nights later. Erle got two black eyes and a badly cut up face in the encounter, but he stayed the limit. He complained that he couldn't keep his mind on the fight because Meyerhoffer kept shouting, "Smile! Smile!" The law forbade the sale of tickets for "fights." The Swede claimed that he was not staging "fights" but genteel calisthenics, and he insisted that his fighters prove the point by incessant simpering. The deputy district attorney summoned Erle and gave him such an eloquent scolding that, in the middle of it, Erle resolved to become a lawyer instead of a prize fighter, and he took a job as a clerk and typist in the deputy district attorney's law office.

The elder Gardner came back from the mines and carried Erle off to Palo Alto for more education. He decided that the only way to educate Erle was to make him live in education, and he placed the boy in the home of J. C. Templeton, principal of the Palo Alto High School. Besides several hundred pupils, the principal had eight children of his own, and one extra boy meant no more to him than one extra grain of dust to a vacuum cleaner. Templeton correctly diagnosed Erle's trouble as excess energy, and he harnessed the boy to a schedule that consumed his energy to the last candlepower. Erle got up early, read Blackstone for two or three hours before breakfast, made school on the run, and left it on the run for a law office, where he typed legal papers until 9:30 P.M., after which he did his homework. On graduating from high school, Erle took a job at twenty dollars a month in a law office at Willows, the goose-hunting center of California. At twenty-one, with both eyes blackened from sparring, he passed his law examinations. He studied the infinitely complicated subject of California irrigation law in the office of

E. E. Keech at Santa Ana, California. In 1912 he married Natalie Talbert, a native of Mississippi. They have a daughter, Mrs. Alan R. McKittrick.

In 1913 Erle hung out his shingle at Oxnard, a town in the sugar-beet section of California, midway between Los Angeles and Santa Barbara. His reception in Oxnard put new life into Erle's underdog complex. The last young lawyer to hit the town was thoroughly disliked, and finally left. He was known in retrospect as "that damn young lawyer," and Erle inherited the title. For a time, his only close friend was a broken-down prize fighter who used him as a sparring partner. Erle was called "the Chinamen's attorney," many of his early clients being Orientals charged with playing fan-tan and chuck-a-luck, selling lottery tickets or hitting the pipe. Having little else to do, Erle put on tremendous legal shows in behalf of his petty offenders. After becoming the recognized Napoleon of the township justice bar, he gained some important clients, and in 1915 he joined Frank Orr, an established lawyer in Ventura, a city of 20,000 and county seat of Ventura County.

Erle was not like Max S. Steuer, the New York legal artist, who said, "I can't think till I have money." Erle did some of his most furious thinking for pauper clients. Ventura still talks of the road-show Sacco-Vanzetti cases which he staged at his own expense on behalf of needy murderers. But his habit of boiling for fees made him disinclined to boil gratis. He was like a prize fighter who puts a price tag on his assault and battery and hates to dissipate it in barrooms, where there are no gate receipts. Erle was ready to fight the opposing lawyer with law, fists, taunts, open abuse and dirty asides, but outside the courtroom he developed the disposition of a woolly lamb.

In spite of the chastening effect of law and business, Erle never wholly ceased to be a Wrong-way Corrigan. He is generally ready to back his notions against the wisdom of the ages. At Palo Alto, in order to show up the culinary authorities, he invented his own food combinations, one of which was a dish consisting of hot waffles, butter, maple sirup, raw oysters and ketchup. Today he thinks the world is grossly imposed on by the undeserved reputation of Martinis, Manhattans and Old-fashioneds. He mixes his own ambiguous appetizers with Mexican ingredients.

The coyote is one of the most disliked members of the animal kingdom. According to Mark Twain, fleas would leave it for a velocipede. Today a coyote sleeps at the foot of Erle's bed at his ranch at Temecula, California.

Authorities on animated nature say rattlesnakes have bad dispositions. That alone was enough to make Erle doubt it. On a hunting trip, Dr. E. K. Roberts, a Ventura dentist and woodsman, thought Erle had gone cuckoo when he heard him babbling away all by himself in a sickening kind of baby talk. He found Erle squatting on his haunches, showering compliments on a rattlesnake and preparing to pet it. The dentist broke up the tête-à-tête by yanking Erle away. Erle was furious. He said that the reptile was a civil little fellow, and that in another moment he would have confounded the authorities by proving that a rattlesnake would accept a pat on the head in the spirit in which it was given. The dentist was not impressed. He had once been bitten by a rattlesnake and was on the side of the authorities.

Erle sometimes lost his chip-on-the-shoulder attitude toward civilization with surprising suddenness. For a long time he had despised golf as a symbol of twentieth-century

One of Gardner's earlier pictures. Some of the "cherubic innocence" Alva Johnston mentions has worn off, but enough remains to indicate the guilelessness Gardner could assume when slipping a fast one over on the D.A.

Pacing the floor of his study, Gardner works out a tough plot.
A secretary says he sometimes does a hundred miles to a book.

Gardner enjoys company at the Rancho del Paisano, but he never lets anything interfere with his work. When there are too many interruptions, he goes by car to his mountain hideaway. There he does his own cooking, works intensively.

Gardner loves this kind of country, where he can work un-molested by the distractions of city-life.

When Gardner feels the need for quick exercise, he takes his bow and arrow, puts in ten or fifteen minutes playing archery-golf or shooting at rovers.

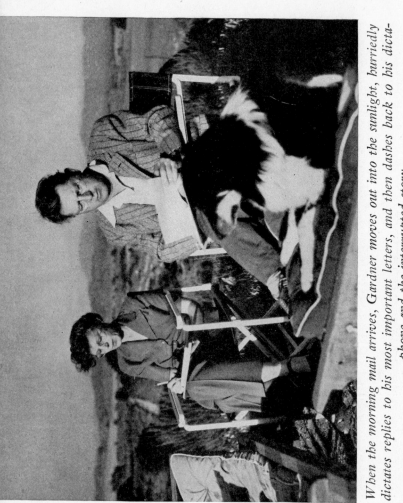

When the morning mail arrives, Gardner moves out into the sunlight, hurriedly dictates replies to his most important letters, and then dashes back to his dictaphone and the interrupted story.

On a Saturday afternoon, the whole office-force rides around the ranch.

When a question as to the location of Gardner property-lines and a war-time scarcity of surveyors posed a dilemma, Gardner resolved it himself. By his own ingenious method, he was able to locate his corners in the almost impenetrable terrain of his mountain ranch three miles away.

It could be he's just interested in the knife "Tony" Ashman, his friend and neighbor, holds. And then again—the exact condition of the edge could be a clue in his next book.

In spite of years of quantity production, Gardner has never been "written out"—largely because he has traveled widely, picking up new objects and ideas with insatiable curiosity. The objects fill his study; the ideas, his books.

Gardner constantly refers to his extensive and varied library.
His vault is packed with priceless books of reference from the
Orient, the South Seas, and South America.

When he leaves his mountain cabin, he carries with him a case
of dictated cylinders, which will later be transcribed by his
secretaries at the main ranch.

A moment of repose at the mountain ranch. When it comes to animals, Gardner is a push-over. He's never been known to speak sharply to any animal—except, possibly, a burro.

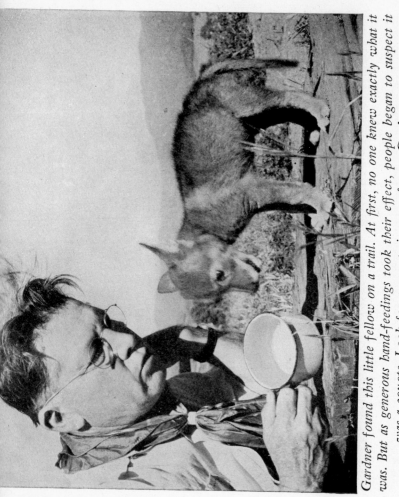

Gardner found this little fellow on a trail. At first, no one knew exactly what it was. But as generous hand-feedings took their effect, people began to suspect it was a coyote. Look for a coyote in some future Gardner story.

Don't accept a bid to move cattle with Gardner unless you can really ride.

This is the laugh triumphant. You'll get it as Gardner tops your full-house with four of a kind—or refutes conclusively your careless denial that black is the same as white.

decay. One of his clients was a sturdy yeoman who rammed his truck into a golfer's roadster and then punched the golfer's nose. Erle won the case by ridiculing the golfer's baggy white knee pants and his impudent pretense that a golfer had any rights that an honest man is bound to respect. A little later Erle was shanghaied to a golf course by an important client. Within a month he had joined two golf clubs and was ballooning all over the landscape in voluminous knickerbockers.

Even after several years at the law, there was still enough revolution left in Erle's system to furnish out a first-class Peck's Bad Boy. He adorned his office with indiscreet art in order to horrify strait-laced visitors. He made a bet with a professional photographer on which could bring home the most demoralizing unposed leg studies. Erle carried off the honors by concealing a small camera in the left front headlight of his automobile and snapping women at close range as they climbed on streetcars. It was the period of tight, ankle-length skirts, and the leg sometimes escaped clear to the knee, exposing a vista of black cotton stocking that would make a satyr blush. Erle's gallery of legoramas was the talk of the town.

He never lost his pro-underdog instinct. Goebbels put him on the Nazi ban in 1939, on the ground that his books glorified the underdog. Erle is probably the only writer that ever discovered underdog characteristics in an agent or a publisher. By all the rules, an author must regard his agent as an incompetent thief and his publisher as a high-class shell-and-pea man. That being the orthodox attitude, Erle has the contrary one. He lives in morbid fear that he is picking the pockets of agents and grinding the faces of publishers.

49

Cornwell Jackson, better known as "Corney," now head of the Hollywood branch of the J. Walter Thompson agency, approached Erle in 1941 with the idea of becoming his Hollywood agent.

"How can you tell what those Hollywood people are going to like?" asked Erle.

"I never have the slightest idea," said Jackson. "I've never been able to understand the first thing about how their minds work."

"You're my agent," said Erle.

Jackson tried to sell Erle's Perry Mason stories to the studios. At an earlier date, Perry had been on the screen and failed to score at the box office. Jackson tried to tell the studios that the Perry Mason pictures had not been well handled and that the lawyer detective could become a knockout in the right hands. Nobody would listen. Perry was spattered with red ink, and Corney might as well have been trying to sell the studios a case of smallpox. The oftener the agent reported "Not a nibble," the more enthusiastic Erle became. He would take Corney out to dinner and exclaim, "That's wonderful!" every time the agent broke bad news. He began to regard Corney as a miracle man. During the war, the agent severed his private business relations and took a Government post. Months after Corney had left him, Erle made a contract to put Perry Mason on the air at a reported price of $50,000 a year. Jackson was taken by surprise when fat checks began to roll in. He cabled Erle, who was then covering the Oakes murder case in the Bahamas for the Hearst papers, saying that he had had nothing to do with the radio contract, was not entitled to a cent and wouldn't accept the checks.

"Cash those checks and shut your trap," Erle cabled back. Corney obeyed like a good soldier.

Erle was a small object on the publishing horizon when he made his first contract with William Morrow and Company. He was the king of the mystery field when the contract expired. Thayer Hobson, head of the Morrow company, told Erle he was entitled to increased royalties and could write his own ticket. Erle called for a stenographer and dictated a new contract providing for the same royalties and allowing the publisher a generous cut in all movie, radio and other Perry Mason rights.

"Don't you know that anybody who read this would say that you were a fool and I was a crook?" demanded Hobson.

"What do we care?" asked Erle.

Erle's belief seems to be that he acted on hardheaded business principles; that the favorable terms would make the publisher eager to advertise and exploit the books. The true interpretation undoubtedly is that Erle suffered from the feeling of being top dog and that his compassion for the downtrodden extends even to publishers.

In 1916 Erle added a political chapter to his variegated biography. Like most of his other experiences, it became the raw material of fiction, giving a lifelike touch to his bustling picture of small-town politics in the mythical Madison City where the mythical District Attorney Douglas Selby operates. An enthusiast for the antiwar policy of Woodrow Wilson, Erle became a member of the State Democratic Central Committee. He made sensational orations and had a severe attack of colic from licking hundreds of stickers bearing the words WILSON'S WISDOM WINS WITHOUT WAR. California's vote elected Wilson.

He carried the state by such a narrow margin that any state central committeeman could figure that he was the real Warwick who personally appointed Wilson to the White House. Erle reveled in that power-behind-the-throne feeling for a time, but he quit politics forever when the United States entered the war less than six months after Wilson had won on the He-Kept-Us-Out-of-War issue. On top of that, Erle had paid county-committee bills to the tune of $150 out of his own pocket and was never able to collect it from the faithful.

Erle was induced to quit the law by Joe Templeton, a son of the Palo Alto principal and now an executive of the Sparks-Withington Company at Jackson, Michigan. Templeton thought Erle was breaking down from overwork and from a typically wrong-headed habit of starving himself for a long period during the preparation and trial of a case, and of gorging for a long period afterward. Templeton had organized the Consolidated Sales Company, which sold automobile accessories. He was specializing in the Gates-Half-Sole Tires, a rubber covering which was cemented upon worn-out tires. Templeton got Erle to drive up to San Francisco with him to look into the business. The afternoon was one of the hottest of the year. The half-soles gave good service under nearly all conditions, but a temperature of 120 and bad roads were too much, and holes were pinched in the inner tubes. Every puncture gave Joe a chance to show off another of his accessories, a marvelous five-minute vulcanizer which heated a gummed rubber patch over a flame and clamped it over the puncture. Six times the tires gave way under the ferocious heat, and each time Joe and Erle did the repair job under the broiling sun. It was a man-killing experience

—just the thing to fill Erle with enthusiasm. At the sixth blowout, he was ready to sign on the spot, and Joe made him president of the company.

Three years at the head of the sales organization taught Erle many things which helped to make him the world's greatest seller of mysteries. On becoming a writer, he knew how to study "reader trends" and to work the literary business on salesmanship principles. One of his pulp editors described him as "a great merchandiser." In 1926 Erle started to switch from Western adventure to detective fiction because his market analysis indicated the trend to the modern type of mystery. Today he is planning to send some of his detective heroes abroad; he senses a trend to foreign backgrounds as a result of the war-stimulated interest in distant lands.

In the accessory business Erle's sales work suffered at first from overenthusiasm. One of the items handled by Templeton was the $150 Kimball Six-speed Transmission. "You can drive over the tops of buildings with it," was the slogan. By going into the lowest gear and taking each stair at the proper angle, Erle used the six-speed transmission to climb courthouse and city-hall steps. Showing off to a prospective customer, he once rode up a flight of stairs to a church door, just as it opened to let out a wedding party, whereupon Erle veered off and gracefully descended. After he had paraded up and down the steps of a public library for another prospect, Erle looked around for an impressive stunt to clinch the sale. He noticed a low sea wall on the other side of which were the mud flats of San Francisco Bay. He headed for it. The prospect screamed protests, but Erle paid no attention. He loved to hear those nervous outcries from people who didn't know what impossible things the six-speed transmission could accomplish. Erle took the sea wall in his stride and expected to execute figure eights in the mud flat on the other side, but the car bogged down over the wheel tops. Erle suddenly became conscious that the prospect had been screaming that it wasn't an ordinary mud flat, but a sewage-disposal area. Erle rattled on amiably in the hope of giving the impression that nothing in particular had happened. But he was a little excited under the surface. He accidentally dropped a heavy crank on the prospect's bunion, and the man became hysterical with pain. As Erle's flow of cheerful conversation continued, the prospect shouted, "Don't talk to me! Don't say another word!"

Erle gave the man a sidelong glance of jovial camaraderie and got ready to strike a few more notes on the theme that everything was progressing splendidly.

The prospect snatched up the crank and cried, "One more word and I'll brain you!"

Erle sighed, waded back to dry land and telephoned to Don Kimball, who came out with salvage apparatus. The prospect's greatest ambition in life at the moment was never to hear Erle's voice again, and he drove away with Kimball. Erle arrived at Consolidated headquarters just as Kimball, no mean salesman, was signing up the prospect for a large order of six-speed transmissions.

By frantic enterprise, Joe and Erle made the Consolidated one of the fastest-growing businesses in the West. They traveled from town to town giving personal instruction to salesmen and mechanics in the use of their accessories. When they invaded a new community, they put on stirring promotion campaigns. For example, they would hire a horde of schoolboys to take note of the condition of the tires of parked cars and take the license numbers. Then they could look up each owner's name, and write him a personal letter saying they had happened to observe that his left front tire or his right rear tire was pretty badly worn and suggesting that he drop around and have 2000 miles added to its life by a Gates Half-sole.

The reputation of the Consolidated as a business-getter became such that a large Eastern manufacturer, in negotiating to make the Consolidated its sole Western agent, stipulated that Templeton should make a survey and tell the manufacturer what was wrong with his business policies. Templeton was too busy. He wired that Consolidated was sending "our president" to make the survey. Erle was a comparatively green hand at the time, and he protested vigorously, but Templeton forced him to make the trip. Erle looked wise and said little as the manufacturer described his troubles and showed him around the plant.

"Get me a stenographer," said Erle finally.

The secretary of the sales manager was assigned to take his dictation. After vain efforts to think up an opening sentence, Erle suggested that they adjourn somewhere for a cocktail. After the second cocktail, the secretary started to tell what an awful run-around her boss was getting. Erle listened for a while, then ordered dinner and continued to listen. Late in the evening, Erle dictated a long report calling for the adoption of a simple, clear-cut policy that would abolish interdepartmental politics, friction and confusion. While Erle was on his way back to California, Templeton received a telegram from the president of the company, lavishing praise on Erle's report and saying that every recommendation had been put into effect.

A year or two later, Templeton met the president of

the company, who said, "We took your president for a country lawyer and didn't think he knew beans. We were stunned when he gave us an absolutely masterful report. It would take an ordinary business analyst a month to learn what he picked up in three hours."

After that, Erle got several other chances to diagnose sick businesses, and he began to think that his true vocation was that of a business analyst. Late in 1920 Erle's own business got sick so fast that, while he could diagnose the ailments perfectly, there was no time to apply remedies. Joe and Erle had opened branches all over the West. They were making money at one time at a rate of more than $100,000 a year and were thinking of selling out and retiring to lives of ease. The buyers' strike of 1920 gave them a rude awakening. The Consolidated had overexpanded and was unable to cope with near-panic conditions. In 1921 Erle rejoined the law firm of Sheridan, Orr, Drapeau and Gardner on a basis of entire freedom from routine work, enabling him to devote all his time to trials and interesting legal tangles.

The law business thrived, but Erle was discontented. In the salesmanship field he had been continually on the move, and this revived his love of a roving life. Back at the law again, he rebelled against bondage to office hours and court calendars. He decided that the only do-as-you-damn-please occupation in the world was that of grinding out fiction, and he started off in 1923 with *The Shrieking Skeleton*.

The Serpent's Coils, the second story Erle sold to *Black Mask*, caused him to be considered a public menace in Ventura. As usual in Gardner fiction, this had a legal angle. It starts with the heroine making a new will in order to disinherit her husband because she shrewdly conjectures that that tarantula didn't get into her bed by accident. Her husband, a naturalist, owns the finest collection of deadly spiders and snakes in America. His wife explains to him that, under the new will, it would be a mistake for him to unleash his homicidal fauna on her, since her death leaves him broke and her continued existence assures him a modest income. But her husband explains that she has overlooked one all-important point—that, if she promptly goes stark, staring mad, the will is no good. He then breaks open a few cases of scorpions, cobras and Gila monsters, locks her in the room with them and admonishes her that, if she keeps perfectly still, they will not attack her, and she has nothing to lose but her mind. By a surprise twist, she escapes through a sliding door in the ceiling, traps her husband among his rarest assassins and leaves him to his fate.

The fact became known in Ventura that Erle was writing for *Black Mask* under the name of Charles M. Green. Swelling with local pride, a stenographer bought the January 1, 1924, issue, which contained *The Serpent's Coils*. Halfway through the story, she began to scream at the top of her lungs and had to be taken to the hospital in an ambulance.

ONE AFTERNOON IN 1913 a cherub-faced boy lawyer was pacing the floor in his office at Oxnard, California. Erle was in his freshman year as a lawyer, but he had already won his spurs in petty-larceny circles in Oxnard. An elderly lawyer, too busy to bother with small fry, had turned over the tag end of his practice to the twenty-four-year-old newcomer. From the first, Erle defended vagrants, Peeping Toms and chicken thieves as if they were great statesmen impeached for high crimes and misdemeanors.

Erle wasn't aware of it in 1913, but the local court was his literary testing laboratory. Every time he thought up a new monkey wrench to throw into the legal machinery at Oxnard, he was thinking up a plot complication for future use in fiction. Most of his weird maneuvers in his early law practice became surprise twists in the 10,000,000 words which he was later to write for book publishers and pulp magazines.

Erle paced the floor that afternoon because he was in danger of losing prestige in petty-crimes circles. A brilliant Los Angeles practitioner had just acquitted a Chinese lottery-ticket seller of Oxnard by sheer magic. Then he had gone back to Los Angeles, leaving Erle to defend twenty other Chinese accused of selling lottery tickets. There was no defense. Erle faced the prospect of making a pitiable contrast with the Los Angeles wizard.

58

The metropolitan courtroom star, Paul Schenck, had won the case by musical-comedy methods. He had a Chinese assistant who suddenly became wildly excited and burst into ear-piercing singsong. Then Schenck became wildly excited and chimed in with shrill singsong of his own. Everybody was as startled as if a crew of bagpipers had opened a serenade in the courtroom. When all eyes were concentrated on him, the Chinese assistant tapped the lottery ticket several times with his index finger and squealed gleefully. Schenck studied the ticket intently and gave a triumphant cackle.

"Now, sir," said Schenck, addressing the prosecution witness, "I ask you to look very carefully at this ticket and tell the jury whether you are quite certain that this is exactly the same ticket that you purchased from the defendant."

The witness was convinced that Schenck and the Chinese had made some big discovery and were about to trap him. He refused to say positively whether the ticket was the right one or not, and the jury brought in a verdict of not guilty.

Schenck couldn't talk Chinese. He had merely given an imitation of it for moral effect on the witness. A perfectionist himself, Erle later mastered the language and learned to stage his own phony-discovery scenes in honest Chinese dialect. But even if he had been able to talk Chinese in 1913, he couldn't have used the Los Angeles lawyer's trick over and over again in the twenty pending cases. Erle paced the floor for four hours in the hope of inventing a legal razzle-dazzle that would save the day. His competitive spirit was on fire. He was determined to make a showing equal to that of the legal Napoleon from Los Angeles.

Suddenly the moon-faced young barrister stopped in his tracks. An idea had popped into his head. He called in the leader of the Oxnard Chinese, unofficially known as the "Mayor of Chinatown," and talked to him for several minutes in pidgin English.

"Got it straight?" asked Erle finally.

The mayor nodded vigorously and hurried away.

Chinatown was a scene of frantic activity that night. It was as peaceful as a Quaker village on the following morning.

At noon an out-of-town detective arrived in Oxnard and picked up a Chinese who was booked as Ah Lee. The prosecutor had twenty cases and planned to bring the defendants into court at his leisure. At the station the Chinese prisoner gave a friendly greeting to a deputy sheriff who was permanently stationed in Oxnard. This deputy was regarded as a mental giant because he could distinguish one Chinese from another, but he had been kept in the background during the anti-lottery crusade because the Chinese could recognize him at a great distance. The deputy was sulky. He felt that the authorities had pointedly gone over his head. When he found that the prisoner had been booked as Ah Lee, he laughed an I-told-you-so sort of a laugh.

"I guess the drinks are on you," he told the out-of-town detective. "That's not Ah Lee."

"That certainly is Ah Lee," said the detective. "I bought a ticket from him a week ago, and I just arrested him at Ah Lee's laundry."

"If that's Ah Lee, I'm your wife's grandmother," said

60

the deputy. "I've known Ah Lee for ten years. He does my Sunday shirts. This is Wong Duck, the butcher."

"But I tell you he was running the laundry," said the detective. "He was bossing the others around. What would a butcher be doing running a laundry?"

"Who knows why a Chinaman does anything?" asked the deputy.

The out-of-town detective identified another man, from whom he said he had purchased a lottery ticket the week before, as Ho Ling, the grocer.

"He's Ong Hai Foo, the druggist," said the deputy. "Ong's the biggest dealer in dried-lizard medicine in Southern California."

"But I tell you he was running Ho Ling's grocery when we arrested him," said the out-of-town detective. "He was waiting on customers. Why would a druggist be selling vegetables?"

The deputy grunted contemptuously and went out to look over Chinatown for himself. He found the place all scrambled up. Every Chinese shopkeeper was running some other man's shop. The deputy finally straightened out all the identities, but the prosecuting attorney shook his head.

"There's been a lot of monkey business going on here," he said, "but we can't get convictions when our witness starts by picking out the wrong men. All the cases will have to be dropped."

That was exactly the result Erle had aimed at. The idea that popped into his head as he paced the floor was that of putting every Chinese businessman in some other man's place of business.

Wong Duck had been booked as Ah Lee. Since the charge was on the record, the case had to be disposed of in court.

It was quietly dismissed. The Oxnard *Courier* described the incident under the headline:

WONG DUCK IS WRONG DUCK

The authorities were sore. The anti-lottery crusade had been planned on business principles. It should have been good for a couple of thousand bucks' worth of fines to the Ventura County treasury. Instead, the county was stuck for special detective expenses, and the Ventura County taxpayers were notorious for counting every penny spent by their officials. The authorities denounced Erle's Chinatown shake-up as a low scheme to obstruct justice.

"The authorities have no right," replied Erle, "to try to convict a man unless they can make an honest identification of him. Their detective was identifying street addresses instead of human beings. All I did was to arrange a fair test of his ability to identify these defendants. It's not my fault that he flunked it."

The boy lawyer soaked the Chinese the colossal fee of $100, and they paid it without a murmur. They recognized that, in killing twenty cases by a simple memory test, he had outshone the celebrated acquitter from Los Angeles.

Erle didn't realize it at the time, but in his Chinatown shake-up he was salting away thousands of dollars' worth of literature for future consumption. The Chinatown bamboozlement pops up in many disguises in the Erle Stanley Gardner mysteries. It is an instructive example of how big literary crops can be harvested from unimportant-looking seeds of experience.

It was easy to detect the pattern of the Chinatown shake-up in a fast play by Erle's famous lawyer detective, Perry Mason, in *The Case of the Howling Dog*. Perry's innocent client, Mrs. Bessie Forbes, gets herself involved in a way that makes her look like a murderess. She is guilty of the unpardonable carelessness of leaving a handkerchief powerfully scented with Vol de Nuit in a taxicab which takes her to the scene of the crime. Perry's experience teaches him that the taxi driver will probably not be able to make an honest identification of Mrs. Forbes, but that on the witness stand he will say, "That's the woman," with a ring of conviction that will impress the jury. So Perry selects an actress named Mae Sibley, dresses her like Mrs. Forbes, scents her with Vol de Nuit and sends her to claim the handkerchief before the taxi driver gets the news of the murder. Sniffing the Vol de Nuit, the man unhesitatingly turns Mrs. Forbes' handkerchief over to Mae Sibley. At the trial, the driver dramatically identifies Mrs. Forbes as the woman who lost the handkerchief and came back for it.

"Mae Sibley, stand up!" thunders Perry Mason.

In the scene that follows, the taxi driver is destroyed as a witness against Mrs. Forbes.

Literature has reveled in mistaken identity since the beginning of time. The long-lost twin brother has seen literary service for twenty-five or thirty centuries. Shakespeare nearly killed the whole mistaken-identity business by hurling a double set of doubles at his audience in *A Comedy of Errors*. Other writers mixed the babies up in their cradles until the thing became a bore. In his variations on the Chinatown shake-up, Erle reinstated the mistaken-identity device on a reasonable basis. It is entirely plausible to ring in a fake double for the purpose of demoralizing a shaky witness. This method has none of the ancient nonsense of palming off a pretender on wives, sweethearts and boyhood chums, but it still produces the good old plot complications of mistaken identity.

Erle's $100 Oxnard case paid him another dividend in *The Case of the Counterfeit Eye*, in which Perry Mason causes an actress to double for a runaway witness. The judge and district attorney threaten Perry with contempt and disbarment, but forget about it when the trick miraculously leads to the unmasking of the real murderer.

Alexander Woollcott said that the first law of literature was that any writer was a fool who didn't sell the same thing under different forms to at least three different editors. Erle used the Chinatown formula a third time in *Owls Don't Blink*, one of the Donald Lam-Bertha Cool mysteries written by Erle under the name of A. A. Fair. In this story, a young woman knows that she hasn't a chance of defending a divorce case or getting alimony because of the mass of evidence which her wealthy husband has framed up against her. So she sublets her apartment to a girl friend who is carefully made up to resemble her. An unsuspecting subpoena server serves the divorce complaint at the right address but on the wrong woman, and a masterful set of complications ensues.

Erle has proved that any smart lawyer has a library of unborn literature in his system. What he did with one $100 case makes it appalling to think what could be done in the dark-and-bloody department of letters by legal giants like Governor Dewey, Charles Evans Hughes, Homer Cummings, John W. Davis and Jerry Giesler.

Lawyers have made their mark in literature from the time of Moses to the present, but few of them have had the enterprise to novelize their learning. The late Arthur Train with his remarkable "Mr. Tutt" and Erle Stanley Gardner are among the very few Americans of this century who have systematically used fiction to cash in on their courtroom experiences. Sir Walter Scott was a practicing lawyer for several years and a court clerk for twenty-five years. His stirring trial scenes in Guy Mannering give a hint of what he could have achieved if the Erle Stanley Gardner formula had been known in his day. Fearing that novel writing would damage his legal standing, Scott tried to make a secret of his authorship. He was probably well advised. The best-selling American-lawyer novelist before Gardner was Lew Wallace, author of Ben Hur. Wallace told his fellow Hoosier, Booth Tarkington, that his success as a writer almost ruined him as a lawyer. All that an opposing lawyer had to do was to say, "I believe my opponent has written a book," and the courtroom would roar with laughter, and Wallace's usefulness to his client would be practically at an end. Erle's former partners say that Erle is pining for trial work, and they predict that he will be back in the harness as soon as they get a big swashbuckling case for him. It would be interesting to see whether it will disturb Erle's equilibrium to have opposing lawyers fling Perry Mason in his teeth.

Erle never literally translates a law case into a mystery. He hasn't sold more than 20,000,000 books solely because he knows some law. The chief effect of his twenty years of legal practice has been to give him a cocksure aggressiveness in tackling all kinds of problems and a smooth skill in solving them. Perry Mason and Erle's other lawyer detectives have the surefootedness of mountain goats in leaping from crag to crag in the legal Bad Lands of Erle's imagination. An old law case is often the thing that starts

65

the fiction machinery in operation, but the plaintiff, witnesses and defendants are soon mixed up in freshly invented entanglements, and the original issues fade out of the scenario. Then, from time to time, the characters fight their way into scrapes which parallel situations from Erle's law practice or reading, and chunks of experience enter the fictional mosaic.

The jumbling up of Chinatown put Erle in high favor with the Chinese. They regarded it as the work of an Oriental type of brain and began to feel a spiritual kinship for the young lawyer. The Mayor of Chinatown told Erle that a learned philosopher had been hired to look him up and that an astonishing discovery had been made.

"Three incarnations ago," said the mayor, "you were a Chinese."

An immediate effect of the Chinatown shake-up was to increase Erle's unpopularity with local officials. After he had won some other cases by legal sleight-of-hand, the official climate became progressively unhealthy for him.

"They say you don't play fair," a client told Erle, "and they're going to run you out of town by throwing your clients in jail until they agree to get some other lawyer."

Some clients quit Erle, saying they had been threatened with daily arrest. Oxnard officials have always denied that they ever schemed to "run Erle out of town." They say that most of his clients were in daily need of police attention and got it as a matter of routine rather than as part of any concerted drive against Erle. The truth is pretty well lost in the mists of antiquity. The important point is that Erle believed that the engines of society had ganged up on him. It gave him the rampaging emotional energy that comes from a sense of fighting against enormous odds.

It furnished Erle with hundreds of thousands of dollars' worth of literary capital.

One of the most incident-packed campaigns of Erle's Oxnard career was the Soo Hoo Yow case. It wasn't worth more than a small fine or a lecture from the bench at the outset. But Erle's blood was up, and Oxnard's blood was up. They carried on a knock-down-and-drag-out fight for weeks through lower, higher and intermediate courts to the accompaniment of high politics and earth-shaking scandals. Although the matter involved was only a twenty-five-cent lottery ticket, the Soo Hoo Yow case is of special interest in proving that Perry Mason came honestly by his cunning, resourcefulness and never-say-die spirit.

Soo Hoo Yow was guilty. The case against him was ironclad. The authorities hadn't identified a street address this time. They had caused a detective with a camera eye to etch Soo Hoo Yow's features on his brain. It is a legal maxim that, when there is no defense, the only thing to do is to try the judge, the jury or the opposing counsel. Erle tried the city of Oxnard. He asserted that Soo had not offended the peace and dignity of Oxnard by selling a lottery ticket, but by having Erle Stanley Gardner for a lawyer.

The judge rapped with his gavel. "That's irrelevant," he said.

Erle said he was ready to produce a witness who, hiding in a closet, had overheard an offer from a police official to let Chinatown run wide open, provided that Chinatown would fire Erle, get a new lawyer and have a man plead guilty at stated intervals, so that Oxnard would receive a just rake-off in fines from the lottery business.

There was great public excitement. City trustees, leading

citizens and big taxpayers flocked to the courtroom. After a viciously fought trial, the jury disagreed. A second trial resulted in a verdict of guilty.

Soo was convicted under an Oxnard city ordinance. A California statute permitted cities to enact ordinances, provided they didn't conflict with state laws. In order to be sure there was no such conflict, Oxnard's ordinance was drawn up in the exact language of the state law. That was exactly where the conflict came in, according to Erle. He argued that Oxnard was trying to compete with the state and to oust the state from its own jurisdiction. Erle's reasoning was upheld in the higher court, the ordinance declared null and void and the proceedings against Soo Hoo Yow thrown out the window.

Oxnard's ego was bruised. It was out to get Soo Hoo Yow if there was any law left on the Pacific Coast. Erle anticipated that Oxnard's next move in this grudge fight would be to re-arrest Soo under the state antilottery law. Conviction appeared inevitable, and, if the sword of justice was wielded in Oxnard, it would descend with great violence on poor Soo. Soo had cost the municipality hundreds of dollars and untold mortification. It would probably take a fine of several hundred dollars, plus a jail sentence, to appease Oxnard.

Erle was working on a counter maneuver before Soo was rearrested. The good old once-in-jeopardy theory leaped into his mind, but he dismissed it for the reason that it was pretty well established that a man was not legally placed in jeopardy by being tried under an unconstitutional law. Soon another beautiful Oriental trick occurred to Erle. He decided to put Soo in jeopardy and then spring the once-in-jeopardy defense.

68

Erle bundled Soo into his car, took him to Ventura and called on Township Justice Knox. He told the justice he had got Soo off on a technicality, but that, in solitary meditation on the subject, he had decided that Soo was guilty and that Soo ought to pay his debt to society. Erle signed a complaint charging Soo with doing exactly what Oxnard had charged him with doing. Justice Knox was ignorant of the bloodthirsty vendetta in Oxnard. Seeing Erle's big innocent eyes and altar-boy face, he thought he was dealing with the preposterously sensitive conscience of a sainted young member of the bar. He accepted a plea of guilty and fined Soo fifteen dollars.

A silence like that of the confessional had brooded over the proceeding before Justice Knox. News of it didn't reach Oxnard. Soo was duly rearrested there under the state law. The Soo Hoo Yow case had become the *Abie's Irish Rose* of Oxnard, and there was standing room only when it came up in court again. Erle pleaded once in jeopardy. That was just what the prosecutor had expected, and he had a mass of authorities to prove that trial under an unconstitutional ordinance didn't constitute jeopardy.

Erle started to interrupt, but the judge said, "Sit down. Your turn will come later."

Erle took a malicious delight in letting his adversary pour on precedents and decisions for an hour and a half.

When the prosecutor sat down, Erle said, "I didn't raise the question of once in jeopardy on that ground. I raised it because the defendant has been tried, convicted and fined under the state law."

"When, where and before whom?" demanded the prosecutor.

"Before Justice Knox at Ventura on August 30, 1915."

"Who swore out the complaint?"

"I did."

By this time all the veteran fans of the Soo Hoo Yow case were buzzing with excitement.

"How much was he fined?" demanded the prosecutor.

"Fifteen dollars," said Erle.

The courtroom howled with laughter.

Erle had previously been called Chong Tzee T'oy, which means "the little lawyer." From this time on, he was known to the Oxnard Chinese as Tai Chong Tzee, which means "the great counselor."

After his first $100, Erle never set a price on his services to the Chinese. On the completion of a case, the mayor would always hand over a fee that was beyond the young lawyer's sanguine dreams of avarice. Because they lived in the midst of alarms and might need emergency advice at any moment, the Chinese kept Erle under a friendly espionage. Once when Mrs. Gardner left Oxnard to visit relatives, they picked the lock of the house, and Erle found a Chinese banquet all cooked for him when he went home in the evening. That was repeated on nearly every similar occasion. The Chinese watched over Erle in other ways. In 1921, when the buyers' strike crippled a business venture of his, he was in financial straits. He received a letter from the cashier of a bank stating that a considerable sum had been deposited to his credit by Chinese who were unknown to the bank. When Erle had used this up, an additional sum was mysteriously deposited. He never did learn the identity of his benefactors.

The study of Chinese history became one of Erle's chief hobbies. He has drawn on his Chinese lore and experience for one novel, *Murder Up My Sleeve,* and for scores of novelettes. On a trip to China in 1931 he was received like a visiting potentate and accorded the unparalleled honor of admission to the Temple of the Passionate Buddha, one of the most strictly forbidden spots in Asia.

Erle's legal science was cross-fertilized by two other sciences—boxing and salesmanship. All three produced important literary by-products. Erle's sparring professors taught him that the whole art of prize fighting consisted of landing punches where they were least expected. Erle made a systematic effort to apply pugilistic philosophy to the law. He hated to try a case on the obvious issues; he always aimed at working his facts into an unexpected picture or digging up a surprise legal theory. His mentors in the sales business taught him to regard law cases as merchandise to be sold to judges and juries. Some of the incidents in the Perry Mason and other Gardner mysteries originated in boxing and salesmanship, went through an incubation stage in Erle's law practice and eventually hatched out into literature.

In *The Case of the Rolling Bones*, for example, the basis for one lively scene was a pep talk on salesmanship, which later played a part in a legal argument, then lay dormant for nineteen years, and finally blossomed out into fiction. The legal argument was part of the suit of Aranetta Hill against Oxnard. Erle felt that his law points were weak and that he was going to lose the case on appeal.

"Never mind the law points," said Joe Templeton, Erle's partner in a sales business. "The law points don't count. Study the psychology of the judges. Do a selling job on them."

Erle took this to heart. He found three aged judges on the bench at Sacramento, and decided to sell them the idea that the younger generation didn't appreciate the older generation.

Aranetta Hill was a very old woman. In 1880 she had planted fifty-five walnut trees with her own hands along a road on her own property. She presented the road to Oxnard with the stipulation that the trees should never be cut down. In 1919, Oxnard, claiming the stipulation was no good, proposed to cut down the trees in order to widen the road. Mrs. Hill hired Erle to save the trees. He lost the decision in the lower court and took an appeal. Addressing the old-timers on the appeals bench, Erle hammered away at the theory that the rising generation failed to appreciate the great things that had been done for the community by the old-timers. Then he told a moving story of the young, thriving city of Oxnard's treatment of its aged benefactress. The three aged jurists decided in Erle's favor on every point.

Perry Mason fights this battle of the generations all over again in the *Rolling Bones* mystery. Perry's client is an old man who is put away in a sanitarium by young relatives to prevent him from remarrying. Perry brings the matter before old Judge Treadwell. A medical expert testifies that the uncle is senile. Old Judge Treadwell bristles at the word. The medical expert says that the uncle has an *arcus senilis*, or white crescent, in the eyes, and that this is a sign of senility.

"Similar to the white-crescent shape in the eye of his honor, Judge Treadwell?" inquires Perry.

The medical expert goes to pieces. Judge Treadwell proclaims that he has had the so-called *arcus senilis* for more than twenty years, denounces the young relatives as greedy upstarts, orders the immediate release of the uncle and starts to investigate the medical expert, with the idea of putting him in jail as a public enemy. The judge's investigation is crossed up by a few decorative homicides which start the case moving in a new direction.

Double or Quits, a mystery written by Erle under the pseudonym of A. A. Fair, contains an idea with a Cinderella history. The idea had a humble early existence in prize-ring lore, and underwent some severe drudgery in the law before it finally luxuriated into fiction. It started with Erle's search for the surprise punch. He had been hired by the family of William Magby, of Ventura, to sue an insurance company for double indemnity. Magby had attempted suicide by taking strychnine and jabbing his throat with bedsprings. He had threatened to kill himself by breathing carbon monoxide, and he was actually found dead in his garage with the garage doors closed and the auto motor running. The beneficiaries were not entitled to double indemnity if the death was a suicide. They weren't entitled to double indemnity unless the death resulted from "accidental means." "Accidental means" is a joker phrase; it doesn't mean the same as "accidental death." For example, the courts held that an insurance company didn't have to pay double indemnity in the case of a pallbearer who dropped dead from a heart attack caused by the weight of the coffin. The pallbearer suffered an "accidental death," but it didn't result from "accidental means," since the pallbearer had knowingly acted as a pallbearer. William Magby's death might have been an accident, but it didn't result from "accidental means," according to the insurance company, since Magby had chosen to work in his garage with a motor running and the doors closed. Erle's magic punch in this case was the weather report of Los Angeles county on the day of Magby's death. It showed that there had been a fairly brisk wind. Erle argued that Magby might have left the garage doors open and that the wind might have blown them shut. That could have produced death by full-fledged "accidental means." The jury gave its verdict in Erle's favor, and the higher courts sustained it. The Magby case was good for about forty pages in *Double or Quits*.

Erle has stated that in his more than 10,000,000 words of fiction he has only once been caught dead to rights in a legal blunder. He carelessly allowed a beneficiary under a will to act as witness to the will. He received countless letters on the subject and always candidly acknowledged his shame. Lawyer fans of Erle's have complained bitterly of some of his other legal propositions, but Erle has defended them as good working theories that had at least a fighting chance of being sustained by the top tribunals.

A working theory of this kind, which makes its appearance in *The Case of the Turning Tide*, is one of Erle's triple plays—Marquis of Queensberry to Blackstone to Gramps Wiggins, Erle's wayward grandfather detective. In a complicated estate contest at Ventura, Erle had felt the necessity of inventing a bolo punch or a La Blanche swing that would catch the adversary completely off guard. The estate had been owned by a wealthy farmer. A hired man had murdered the farmer first, the wife second, and their only child third. He confessed and was hanged. The estate was put through the courts, on the theory that the wife had inherited the estate on the farmer's death and that the child had inherited the estate on the mother's death. It was, therefore, the child's estate that was being distributed. The farmer's relatives included

74

"whole brothers" and "half brothers." The half brothers would have shared in the estate if the farmer had died last, but under the California law the half brothers had no share in the estate of the child. The half brothers went to several lawyers, who told them they were out of luck. Then they went to Erle. His first impulse was to tell them they were out of luck, but, instead, he followed his usual course of hunting for the unexpected punch, and he found one. He came up with the theory that the only evidence that the farmer died first had been hanged. He said that the murderer's confession had not been made under oath and couldn't be used as testimony in the estate litigation. Since there was, therefore, no legal evidence as to who died first, Erle asserted that the law relating to a "public calamity" governed the case and that the public-calamity law assumed that the adult male died last. The public-calamity law was intended to cover the death of whole families in shipwrecks, but Erle contended that it applied to multiple murders.

This out-of-nowhere wallop scared the whole brothers into making a substantial cash settlement with the half brothers, so that the issue didn't have to be decided by the courts. Nearly twenty years later Erle hit the literary jack pot by using the public-calamity theory in the *Turning Tide* murders.

The Case of the Empty Tin contains an incident which further illustrates the mysterious process by which literature is made. This particular incident was born in legal knowledge, licked into shape by an embarrassing personal experience and then freely translated into fiction.

Perry Mason's client in the *Empty Tin* imbroglio is one Elston Karr. A shooting takes place on the floor below

Karr's apartment. Karr is hiding out from his enemies and can't afford to have his whereabouts known. He calls in Perry Mason to keep his name out of the papers. There is a popular superstition to the effect that a certain black art can be used to keep a man's name out of the papers. In actual practice, the more a man strives to keep his name out of the papers the more frequently and disastrously it gets in. By a simple device, however, the dexterous Perry Mason succeeds in keeping his client out of the limelight. Perry tells the police that Karr knows nothing about the shooting except that he heard two shots. The police instantly lose interest in the man. Karr asks why Perry said there were two shots when there was only one.

"When you tell a man like Lieutenant Tragg to keep your name out of the papers, it doesn't mean a damn thing," Perry explains. "But if you give him testimony which is at variance with the case which he is working up, then he's certain to see your name is kept out of the papers."

"Why?" asks Karr.

Perry explains that the police don't like to play into the hands of the defense by focusing attention on a man who contradicts the prosecution's witnesses.

There are mystery authors who have subtle and fantastic imaginations. Pure imagination, however, doesn't produce funny business like Perry Mason's two shots for one; it takes experience and technical know-how. Erle's legal scuffles had taught him that prosecutors hated to rely on garrulous and imaginative witnesses. His general knowledge on the subject received a strenuous workout in a personal jam that Erle got into after he had acquitted one big-city gangster and saved the neck of another in a Ventura murder case. This case gave him considerable prestige in the underworld, and, as he was writing crime stuff for pulp magazines, he decided to make a first-hand study of gang life. He was warmly received into some of the lowest circles in the country. A talent for fortune-telling made him the valued adviser of gun molls.

One day the authorities swooped down on Erle and started to question him about certain gang activities. Erle couldn't claim that a writer's local color is a professional secret. He was still a practicing attorney, and it would have hurt him to go before a grand jury in a gangster case. Erle started to be noncommittal and evasive. Then a better idea struck him, and he became helpful, loquacious, full of startling statements and wild surmises. The prosecutor dropped him like a hot potato. When Erle's fictional character got into a similar jam, Erle knew just what to do. Erle's and Perry's method of keeping a man's name out of the newspapers is not generally to be recommended, however. When the ordinary man tampers with the facts, he is likely to be thrown into a cell until his mind clears.

BIBLIOGRAPHY

OF ERLE STANLEY GARDNER

CASE OF THE VELVET CLAWS, THE. William Morrow & Co., Inc., New York, 1933; George Harrap & Co., London, 1933, 1934, 1935; Grosset & Dunlap, Inc., New York, 1934, 1940; Pocket Books, New York, 1940; Triangle Books, New York, 1945.

CASE OF THE SULKY GIRL, THE. William Morrow & Co., Inc., New York, 1933; Grosset & Dunlap, Inc., New York, 1934, 1941; George Harrap & Co., London, 1935, 1936, 1937; Pocket Books, New York, 1941; Triangle Books, New York, 1944.

CASE OF THE LUCKY LEGS, THE. William Morrow & Co., Inc., New York, 1934; Grosset & Dunlap, Inc., New York, 1935, 1941; George Harrap & Co., London, 1937; Pocket Books, New York, 1941; Tower Books, Cleveland, 1945; Pocket Books, New York (in *The Perry Mason Case Book*), 1946.

CASE OF THE HOWLING DOG, THE. William Morrow & Co., Inc., New York, 1934; Grosset & Dunlap, Inc., New York, 1935, 1941; Cassell & Co., London, 1937; Pocket Books, New York, 1941; Triangle Books, New York, 1946; Pocket Books, New York (in *The Perry Mason Case Book*), 1946.

CASE OF THE CURIOUS BRIDE, THE. William Morrow & Co., Inc., New York, 1934; Grosset & Dunlap,

Inc., New York, 1935, 1942; Cassell & Co., London, 1936; American Mercury, New York, 1941; Pocket Books, New York, 1942; International Readers League, New York, 1943; Triangle Books, New York, 1946.

CLEW OF THE FORGOTTEN MURDER, THE. William Morrow & Co., Inc., New York (under pseudonym "Carleton Kendrake"), 1935; Cassell & Co., London (under pseudonym "Carleton Kendrake"), 1935; The A. L. Burt Co., New York (under pseudonym "Carleton Kendrake"), 1936; Sun Dial Press, New York, 1942; Triangle Books, New York, 1943; American Mercury, New York, 1943; Pocket Books, New York (in preparation).

CASE OF THE COUNTERFEIT EYE, THE. William Morrow & Co., Inc., New York, 1935; Grosset & Dunlap, Inc., New York, 1936, 1942; Cassell & Co., London, 1937; Pocket Books, New York, 1942; International Readers League, New York, 1943; Triangle Books, New York, 1946.

CASE OF THE CARETAKER'S CAT, THE. William Morrow & Co., Inc., New York, 1935; Grosset & Dunlap, Inc., New York, 1936, 1943; Cassell & Co., London, 1937; Pocket Books, New York, 1942; Tower Books, Cleveland, 1946.

THIS IS MURDER. William Morrow & Co., Inc., New York (under pseudonym "Charles J. Kenny"), 1935; Methuen & Co., London (under pseudonym "Charles J. Kenny"), 1935, 1939; Grosset & Dunlap, Inc., New York (under pseudonym "Charles J. Kenny"), 1936; Sun Dial Press, New York, 1943; American Mercury, New York, 1943; Tower Books, Cleveland, 1944.

CASE OF THE SLEEPWALKER'S NIECE, THE. William Morrow & Co., Inc., New York, 1936; Cassell & Co., London, 1936, 1938; Grosset & Dunlap, Inc., New York, 1937; American Mercury, New York, 1941; Triangle Books, New York, 1942; Pocket Books, New York, 1944; Tower Books, Cleveland, 1946.

CASE OF THE STUTTERING BISHOP, THE. William Morrow & Co., Inc., New York, 1936; Grosset & Dunlap, Inc., New York, 1937, 1943; Cassell & Co., London, 1937, 1938; International Readers League, New York, 1943; Pocket Books, New York, 1943; Tower Books, Cleveland, 1946.

D.A. CALLS IT MURDER, THE. William Morrow & Co., Inc., New York, 1937; Cassell & Co., London, 1937, 1938; Grosset & Dunlap, Inc., New York, 1938; Triangle Books, New York, 1941, 1942; American Mercury, New York, 1941; Pocket Books, New York, 1944.

CASE OF THE DANGEROUS DOWAGER, THE. William Morrow & Co., Inc., New York, 1937; Cassell & Co., London, 1937, 1939; Grosset & Dunlap, Inc., New York, 1938, 1942; American Mercury, New York, 1942; Triangle Books, New York, 1943; International Readers League, New York, 1943; Pocket Books, New York, 1944; Tower Books, Cleveland, 1945.

CASE OF THE LAME CANARY, THE. William Morrow & Co., Inc., New York, 1937; Cassell & Co., London, 1937, 1939; Grosset & Dunlap, Inc., New York, 1939, 1944; Pocket Books, New York, 1943; Triangle Books, New York (in preparation).

MURDER UP MY SLEEVE. William Morrow & Co., Inc., New York, 1937; Cassell & Co., London, 1938, 1939; Grosset & Dunlap, Inc., New York, 1939; Triangle

Books, New York, 1942; American Mercury, New York, 1942; Tower Books, Cleveland, 1944; Cassell & Co., Melbourne, 1944; Pocket Books, New York, 1946.

CASE OF THE SUBSTITUTE FACE, THE. William Morrow & Co., Inc., New York, 1938; Grosset & Dunlap, Inc., New York, 1939, 1945; Cassell & Co., London, 1940; Pocket Books, New York, 1943; Triangle Books, New York (in preparation).

CASE OF THE SHOPLIFTER'S SHOE, THE. William Morrow & Co., Inc., New York, 1938; Grosset & Dunlap, Inc., New York, 1939, 1942; Cassell & Co., London, 1941; Triangle Books, New York, 1942; Tower Books, Cleveland, 1945; Pocket Books, New York, 1945.

D.A. HOLDS A CANDLE, THE. William Morrow & Co., Inc., New York, 1938; Grosset & Dunlap, Inc., New York, 1940; Cassell & Co., London, 1941; Triangle Books, New York, 1942; American Mercury, 1942; Tower Books, Cleveland, 1944; Pocket Books, New York, 1945.

BIGGER THEY COME, THE (under pseudonym "A. A. Fair"). William Morrow & Co., Inc., New York, 1939; Hamish Hamilton, London (under title "Lam to the Slaughter"), 1939; Grosset & Dunlap, Inc., New York, 1940; Triangle Books, New York, 1942; Pocket Books, New York, 1943.

CASE OF THE PERJURED PARROT, THE. William Morrow & Co., Inc., 1939; Cassell & Co., London, 1939; Grosset & Dunlap, Inc., New York, 1940; Triangle Books, New York, 1944; Pocket Books, New York. 1936; Pocket Books, New York (in *The Perry Mason Case Book*), 1946.

CASE OF THE ROLLING BONES, THE. William Morrow & Co., Inc., New York, 1939; Grosset & Dunlap, Inc., New York, 1940, 1945; Cassell & Co., London, 1940; Tower Books, Cleveland (in preparation); Pocket Books, New York (in preparation).

D.A. DRAWS A CIRCLE, THE. William Morrow & Co., Inc., New York, 1939; Cassell & Co., London, 1940; Grosset & Dunlap, Inc., New York, 1941; American Mercury, New York, 1942; Triangle Books, New York, 1943; Pocket Books, New York, 1945; Tower Books, Cleveland (in preparation).

TURN ON THE HEAT (under pseudonym "A. A. Fair"). William Morrow & Co., Inc., New York, 1940; Detective Book Club, New York, 1940; Hamish Hamilton, London, 1940; Grosset & Dunlap, Inc., New York, 1941; Triangle Books, New York, 1942.

CASE OF THE BAITED HOOK, THE. William Morrow & Co., Inc., New York, 1940; Grosset & Dunlap, Inc., New York, 1941; Cassell & Co., London, 1941; Triangle Books, New York, 1945; Pocket Books, New York (in preparation).

D.A. GOES TO TRIAL, THE. William Morrow & Co., Inc., New York, 1940; Grosset & Dunlap, Inc., New York, 1941; Cassell & Co., London, 1941; Triangle Books, New York, 1944; Pocket Books, New York, 1946.

GOLD COMES IN BRICKS (under pseudonym "A. A. Fair"). William Morrow & Co., Inc., New York, 1940; Grosset & Dunlap, Inc., New York, 1942; Robert Hale & Co., London, 1942; Triangle Books, New York, 1944.

CASE OF THE SILENT PARTNER, THE. William
Morrow & Co., Inc., New York, 1940; Cassell & Co.,
London, 1940; Grosset & Dunlap, Inc., New York, 1941;
Triangle Books, New York (in *The Perry Mason Case
Book*), 1946.

CASE OF THE HAUNTED HUSBAND, THE. William
Morrow & Co., Inc., New York, 1941; Grosset & Dun-
lap, Inc., New York, 1942; Cassell & Co., London, 1942;
Tower Books, Cleveland (in preparation).

SPILL THE JACKPOT! (under pseudonym "A. A. Fair").
William Morrow & Co., Inc., New York, 1941; Grosset
& Dunlap, Inc., New York, 1942; Triangle Books, New
York, 1944.

CASE OF THE TURNING TIDE, THE. William Mor-
row & Co., Inc., New York, 1941; Grosset & Dunlap,
Inc., New York, 1942; Cassell & Co., London, 1942;
Triangle Books, New York (in preparation).

CASE OF THE EMPTY TIN, THE. William Morrow &
Co., Inc., New York, 1941; Detective Book Club, New
York, 1941; Grosset & Dunlap, Inc., New York, 1943;
Cassell & Co., London, 1943.

DOUBLE OR QUITS (under pseudonym "A. A. Fair").
William Morrow & Co., Inc., New York, 1941; Detec-
tive Book Club, New York, 1942; Grosset & Dunlap,
Inc., New York, 1943; Triangle Books, New York, 1946.

D.A. COOKS A GOOSE, THE. William Morrow & Co.,
Inc., New York, 1942; Detective Book Club, New York,
1942; Grosset & Dunlap, Inc., New York, 1943; Cassell &
Co., London, 1943; Triangle Books, New York, 1946.

CASE OF THE DROWNING DUCK, THE. William Morrow & Co., Inc., New York, 1942; Detective Book Club, New York, 1942; Grosset & Dunlap, Inc., New York, 1943; Cassell & Co., London, 1944.

OWLS DON'T BLINK (under pseudonym "A. A. Fair"). William Morrow & Co., Inc., New York, 1942; Grosset & Dunlap, Inc., New York, 1943; Triangle Books, New York (in preparation).

CASE OF THE CARELESS KITTEN, THE. William Morrow & Co., Inc., New York, 1942; Grosset & Dunlap, Inc., New York, 1943; International Readers League, New York, 1943; Cassell & Co., London, 1945.

BATS FLY AT DUSK (under pseudonym "A. A. Fair"). William Morrow & Co., Inc., New York, 1942; Detective Book Club, New York, 1942; Grosset & Dunlap, Inc., New York, 1944; Triangle Books, New York (in preparation).

CASE OF THE SMOKING CHIMNEY, THE. William Morrow & Co., Inc., New York, 1943; Detective Book Club, New York, 1943; International Readers League, New York, 1943; Grosset & Dunlap, Inc., New York, 1944; Cassell & Co., London, 1945.

CASE OF THE BURIED CLOCK, THE. William Morrow & Co., Inc., New York, 1943; Detective Book Club, New York, 1943; Grosset & Dunlap, Inc., New York, 1944; Cassell & Co., London, 1946.

CATS PROWL AT NIGHT (under pseudonym "A. A. Fair"). William Morrow & Co., Inc., New York, 1943; Detective Book Club, New York, 1943; Grosset & Dunlap, Inc., New York, 1945; Tower Books Cleveland (in preparation).

CASE OF THE DROWSY MOSQUITO, THE. William Morrow & Co., Inc., New York, 1943; Detective Book Club, New York, 1943; Grosset & Dunlap, Inc., New York, 1944.

D.A. CALLS A TURN, THE. William Morrow & Co., Inc., New York, 1944; Detective Book Club, New York, 1944; Grosset & Dunlap, Inc., New York, 1945.

CASE OF THE CROOKED CANDLE, THE. William Morrow & Co., Inc., New York, 1944; Detective Book Club, New York, 1944; Grosset & Dunlap, Inc., New York, 1945.

GIVE 'EM THE AX (under pseudonym "A. A. Fair"). William Morrow & Co., Inc., New York, 1944; Detective Book Club, New York, 1944; Grosset & Dunlap, Inc., New York, 1945; Editions for the Armed Services, New York, 1945.

CASE OF THE BLACK-EYED BLONDE, THE. William Morrow & Co., Inc., New York, 1944; Grosset & Dunlap, Inc., New York, 1945; Detective Book Club, New York, 1945; Editions for the Armed Services, New York, 1945.

CASE OF THE GOLDDIGGER'S PURSE, THE. William Morrow & Co., Inc., New York, 1945; Detective Book Club, New York, 1945; Grosset & Dunlap, Inc., New York, 1946; Editions for the Armed Services, New York, 1946. Reproduced on microfilm by Viz, Inc.. New York, 1946.

CASE OF THE HALF-WAKENED WIFE, THE. M. S. Mill Co., Inc., New York, 1945; Detective Book Club, New York, 1945; Editions for the Armed Services, New York, 1945; Grosset & Dunlap, Inc., New York, 1946.

D.A. BREAKS A SEAL, THE. William Morrow & Co., Inc., New York, 1946; Detective Book Club, New York, 1946; Grosset & Dunlap, Inc., New York (in preparation).

CROWS CAN'T COUNT (under pseudonym "A. A. Fair"). William Morrow & Co., Inc., New York, 1946; Detective Book Club, New York, 1946; Grosset & Dunlap, Inc., New York (in preparation).

CASE OF THE BACKWARD MULE, THE. William Morrow & Co., Inc., New York, 1946; Detective Book Club, New York, 1946.

CASE OF THE BORROWED BRUNETTE, THE. William Morrow & Co., Inc., New York, 1946; Detective Book Club, New York, 1947.

TWO CLUES: THE CLUE OF THE RUNAWAY BLONDE and THE CLUE OF THE HUNGRY HORSE. William Morrow & Co., Inc., New York, 1947.

CASE OF THE FAN-DANCER'S HORSE, THE. William Morrow & Co., Inc., New York (in preparation).